LITTLE BOOK OF
VEGETARIANISM

Alexa Kaye

summersdale

THE LITTLE BOOK OF VEGETARIANISM

Text by Abi McMahon

An Hachette UK Company
www.hachette.co.uk

Summersdale Publishers Ltd
Part of Octopus Publishing Group Limited
Carmelite House
50 Victoria Embankment
LONDON
EC4Y 0DZ
UK

www.summersdale.com

Printed and bound in Malta

ISBN: 978-1-78685-773-6

Substantial discounts on bulk quantities of Summersdale books are available to corporations, professional associations and other organisations. For details contact general enquiries: telephone: +44 (0) 1243 771107 or email: enquiries@summersdale.com.

Contents

Introduction

Welcome to *The Little Book of Vegetarianism*. Maybe you've picked this up because you're curious about cutting meat out of your diet; maybe you're already a veggie, or well on your way to becoming one and would like some more background info and inspiration to jazz up your meals. Whatever your reason, this little book is designed to give you bite-sized nuggets of trivia to have up your sleeve to help you talk to people about vegetarianism, understand why people live the lifestyle and consider how it can work for you. There are also lots of recipes and recommendations to enjoy – happy cooking!

BUT FOR THE SAKE OF SOME LITTLE MOUTHFUL OF FLESH, WE DEPRIVE A SOUL OF THE SUN AND LIGHT, AND OF THAT PROPORTION OF LIFE AND TIME IT HAD BEEN BORN INTO THE WORLD TO ENJOY.

PLUTARCH

WHAT VEGETARIANISM MEANS: A BRIEF Q&A

If you've got this far it's pretty likely that you're thinking of becoming vegetarian, or have already made the transition. Good for you! Now is the perfect time to switch to a meat-free lifestyle. If you're wondering how to get started then you've come to the right place!

We now know more about nutrition, so we know how to maintain a healthy diet. The shops are stocking more meat-free food than ever so there is plenty of choice. There is simply buckets of information out there on why vegetarianism is an ethical, healthy and environmentally friendly lifestyle choice and this chapter will help to answer some of your most pressing questions.

WHAT KIND OF VEGETARIAN AM I?

A nice one! But seriously, there are all sorts of different types of diet based on the ethical and healthy exclusion of animal products.

I exclude meat, fish and shellfish from my diet, but still eat eggs and dairy – you're a *lacto-ovo-vegetarian*. This is your commonly spotted vegetarian. Most menu items and food products that market themselves as vegetarian include eggs and/or dairy.

I exclude meat, fish, shellfish and eggs from my diet, but still eat dairy – you're a *lacto-vegetarian*. Eggs are a common source of protein for vegetarians, so be sure to include other protein-rich foods in your diet.

I exclude meat, fish, shellfish and dairy from my diet, but still eat eggs – you're an *ovo-vegetarian*. Dairy products are a good source of calcium so add calcium-fortified alternatives and greens such as kale to your shopping list.

I exclude meat, fish and shellfish from my diet sometimes - you're a *flexitarian*! You may prefer to not eat those products but make exceptions in certain circumstances. (If you have a meat/fish/shellfish meal at least once a week, you're probably still an omnivore.)

I exclude meat, fish, shellfish, dairy and eggs from my diet - you have graduated from the school of vegetarianism and you are now a *vegan*!

WHAT'S WRONG WITH EATING MEAT?

People choose to not eat meat for different reasons. Some people simply don't like the taste or texture, others don't agree with the processes used to rear and kill the animals we eat, or with the principle of killing animals for our benefit at all. Some people recognise that agricultural animal farming hogs a lot of the world's resources, and others are taking advantage of a global food trade that allows them to eat well without needing any animals to die.

WHAT ABOUT FISH?

Eating fish is seen by some as a different kettle of, er, fish to eating meat. After all, fish are caught out at sea and don't have to suffer through some of the cruelties of farming, so it's just like the circle of life, right? Not necessarily. Firstly, some fish *are* farmed, such as carp, salmon or catfish. Secondly, the world's oceans are overfished and fish stock levels are struggling. At least a third of the commercial fishing spots are overfished and no longer able to naturally replenish their stocks, meaning there are fewer fish and the ecosystem is unbalanced. Thirdly, commercial ocean fishing is an inexact craft with tight budget margins and pressing deadlines, so although fishing ships are meant to promptly return sea life, such as dolphins or sharks, to the sea unharmed many suffer in the nets and are left on the deck to drown before being thrown back into the sea. Even fish farms contribute to overfishing, as carnivorous fish are fed with ground-down fish from the sea.

CRUELTY IS ONE FASHION STATEMENT WE CAN ALL DO WITHOUT.

RUE McCLANAHAN

SO AS LONG AS I DON'T EAT MEAT, I'M OK?

Oh heck! Sorry but animal products aren't only found in food. You might want to avoid materials such as suede, fur and leather, which are made from animal skins. Even some food that you might think is safe needs an extra look – chewy or 'gummy' sweets are often made using gelatine, which is boiled down hoof or trotter. (Luckily there are lots of new brands of vegetarian gummy sweets made from ingredients such as pectin or palm gum. Hello fizzy cola bottles!) Some cheeses such as Parmesan, Grana Padano or Gorgonzola use rennet, which is an enzyme from the stomachs of new-born calves so they may be off the menu too. If you're into getting your nails done, you might want to go for acrylics over shellac as that's made using insect secretions (see p.111). A top tip for new vegetarians is to spend a few weeks familiarising yourself with some of the most common sneaky animal products, and scrutinising the ingredients and processes of your favourite food, clothes, bags, shoes etc., because you may be surprised where companies have snuck them in.

CAN ONE PERSON MAKE A DIFFERENCE?

You truly can! Going vegetarian is just a set of small changes that will most likely have only positive effects on you, and which will have a profoundly positive effect on the world around you. Just one example: as a vegetarian, you use far less water (this could be up to a 41 per cent reduction) than someone who eats meat and dairy as you do not support the water-guzzling meat industry. Further, if you think one person going vegetarian doesn't make much difference to animals, think about this: during one year alone, on average, a vegetarian will save the lives of 198 animals through not eating meat. Over ten years, that's 1,980 animals who won't lose their lives. That's no mean feat.

PEOPLE EAT MEAT AND THINK THEY WILL BECOME AS STRONG AS AN OX, FORGETTING THAT THE OX EATS GRASS.

PINO CARUSO

CAN YOU GET EVERYTHING YOU NEED FROM A VEGETARIAN DIET?

Yes, you can! In fact, it couldn't be easier. It's a common misconception that humans need to eat meat in order to fulfil their dietary requirements. The nutrients that we get from meat and fish, such as protein and iron, can be found in loads of widely available foods. It's just a matter of knowing where to look. It's a mistaken belief that if you eat a veggie diet you'll be sad and weak or that you need to eat meat to be active and athletic. A vegetarian diet can even be suitable for professional athletes, such as tennis champion Martina Navratilova and alpine skier Bode Miller. See the chapter 'Essential Nutritional Replacements' (pages 22–36) for more details.

IS A VEGETARIAN DIET HEALTHY?

That depends on you! Some studies have observed a link between a diet that includes a lot of processed meat with obesity, heart disease, diabetes and other illnesses. However, that doesn't mean that a vegetarian diet instantly gives you a head start. A vegetarian diet still allows for delicious, yet unhealthy, food such as chips, pizza, chocolate and cake. You do take a step toward a healthier diet when cutting out meat, as it can be a big source of saturated fat in our diets, but you still have to exercise a bit of discretion when piling up the plate. Studies show that those with the healthiest diets are careful about their daily nutritional intake, regardless of which food groups they are taking them from.

All About Vegetarianism

Rearing, keeping, slaughtering and transporting farm animals for human consumption uses up a lot of resources compared to farming plant-based foods – it takes around 11 times more fossil fuel to produce animal protein than plant protein. Animal agriculture also guzzles far more water; it takes anything between 1.5 and 6 times more water to produce a gram of meat protein than it does a gram of protein from pulses.

IS A VEGETARIAN DIET GOOD FOR THE ENVIRONMENT?

Enjoying a vegetarian lifestyle means boycotting industrial agricultural animal farming, which, for some environmentally conscious eaters, is a plus. Also known as 'intensive animal farming' or 'factory farming', industrial animal agriculture refers to farms that manage vast numbers of livestock to meet the growing demands for meat and dairy produce. Animal agriculture creates around 18 per cent of the world's yearly greenhouse gases and seven football field's worth of land is bulldozed every minute to house farmed animals and grow their grain. So is it worth it? No, actually. The conversion of grain into meat is energy-intensive and the input to output is greatly uneven. On average, it takes 7 kilograms of grain to create 1 kilogram of beef, 4 kilograms of pork or just over 2 kilograms of chicken. Studies suggest that industrial animal agriculture struggles to feed the planet, destroys ecosystems on land as well as in the ocean and is a huge contributor to global warming.

THE QUESTION IS, ARE WE HAPPY TO SUPPOSE THAT OUR GRANDCHILDREN MAY NEVER BE ABLE TO SEE AN ELEPHANT EXCEPT IN A PICTURE BOOK?

DAVID ATTENBOROUGH

ESSENTIAL NUTRITIONAL REPLACEMENTS

A vegetarian lifestyle does require a shift in thinking with regards to your nutritional intake, though on balance most people will find that cutting out meat makes more space for delicious fruits and veggies anyway, which is often a good step towards a healthier diet. The best way to feel good and keep energy levels up while changing your diet is to be conscious about your daily requirements and eat according to those. This chapter will give you tips about the best sources of nutrition.

PROTEIN

'How will I get my protein?' is the one of the main questions on everybody's lips when they cut meat from their diet. Actually, there are a lot of foods available to vegetarians that are rich in protein. Adults are recommended to eat 0.75 g protein a day per kilogram they weigh; for a quick guide to your intake, it's estimated at around 55 g a day for an average man and 45 g for an average woman. Turn the page for some great vegetarian sources of protein and how much protein they contain.

100 g peanuts	25 g
100 g sunflower seeds	23 g
100 g almonds	21.1 g
100 g black beans	21 g
100 g chickpeas	19 g
100 g vegetarian mock meat	15 g (estimate)
100 g walnuts	14.7 g
100 g wild rice	15 g
100 g quinoa	14 g
1 egg	12.5 g
100 g tofu	8.1 g
100 g kidney beans	6.9 g
100 g plain yoghurt	4.8 g
100 g peas	5 g
100 g kale	4 g

THE LOVE FOR ALL LIVING CREATURES IS THE MOST NOBLE ATTRIBUTE OF MAN.

CHARLES DARWIN

ZINC

It's easy to overlook zinc intake when you're trying to balance your meals but it shouldn't be discounted. Although you may not think 'I'm feeling a little unwell, must be my zinc deficiency', that may be the reason; if you are deficient in zinc you are more likely to be susceptible to common illnesses such as colds and the flu. You may also suffer some hair loss and increased acne. Build your zinc levels back up with tofu, black beans, kidney beans, lentils, pumpkin seeds, cashews and peanuts.

CALCIUM

Calcium is good for keeping your bones and teeth strong but adults don't need a great deal to be healthy. You only need to consume 0.7 g calcium a day to fulfil your nutritional requirements. It's common knowledge that milk and cheese are good sources of calcium but if you're flirting with the idea of omitting dairy products from your diet you'll be glad to know that there are plenty of other great sources out there.

90 g hard cheese	0.72 g
200 ml semi-skimmed milk	0.25 g
200 ml calcium-enriched soy milk	0.25 g
150 g natural yoghurt	0.2 g
120 g dried figs	0.2 g
60 g almonds	0.15 g
120 g tofu	0.13 g
200 g broccoli	0.12 g
200 g chickpeas	0.1 g
200 g French beans	0.05 g
200 ml soy milk	0.026 g

THE FUTURE WILL EITHER BE GREEN OR NOT AT ALL.

BOB BROWN

VITAMIN B12

B12 is one of the trickier vitamins to replace when relinquishing meat and fish. You only need 0.024 g of it daily and yet there are only a handful of foodstuffs that contain it. However it's essential to keep our metabolism strong and our brains working well. It might be tempting to turn to tablets but they're not very efficient – only 10 mg of every 500 mg of B12 is absorbed when taken in tablet form. Fortunately for Marmite-loving vegetarians, this is your moment of vindication – fortified yeast extracts are rich in B12. You can also include nutritional yeast in your cooking for when you want a cheesy flavour without all the cheese.

100 g fortified cereals	0.018 g
25 g Cheddar cheese	0.015 g
4 g Marmite	0.006 g
1 egg	0.006 g

I JUST COULDN'T STAND THE IDEA OF EATING MEAT – I REALLY DO THINK THAT [STOPPING] IT HAS MADE ME CALMER.

KATE BUSH

VITAMIN D

While it's true you get vitamin D from being exposed to sunlight, if you live in a cooler country it is likely that you're suffering from a vitamin D deficiency in the winter months. Taking vitamin D tablets does help replenish your vitamin D stores but you may want to ensure that you are also doing the best you can with your diet. Breakfast is a good time to get your vitamin D in, as great vegetarian sources include egg yolks, fortified cereals and non-dairy milks.

IRON

The recommended daily amount of iron in your diet is around 0.08 g a day for men and 0.15 g for women between the ages of 19–50 (post-menopausal women require less iron after their periods stop). Surprisingly, cooking in cast-iron pots, especially acidic foods such as tomato sauce, can increase your intake of iron. Otherwise you can get your iron from a variety of veggies, nuts and seeds.

30 g Weetabix	0.04 g
150 g kidney beans	0.03 g
150 g lentils	0.03 g
30 g almonds	0.01 g
150 g broccoli	0.008 g
100 g dried apricots	0.025 g

All About Vegetarianism

Plant-based iron is known as non-heme iron (which sounds a bit otherworldly). It's slightly harder for the body to absorb than heme iron (from animal products), but consuming vitamin C at the same time can improve your body's absorption rate.

OMEGA-3 FATTY ACIDS

Omnivores usually turn to oily fish to get their omega-3 fatty acids. These acids help regulate cholesterol and aid the healthy development of cell membranes. Although you may have chosen to avoid fish, you can still obtain your omega-3 fatty acids from oils and some nuts, beans and fortified dairy and soy products. There is no recommended daily intake for omega-3, although you can refer to the recommendations for your daily saturated fat intake and ensure omega-3 fatty acids constitute a portion of that.

1 tbsp rapeseed (vegetable) oil	3.9 g
1 tbsp flaxseed oil	2 g
25 g walnuts	13.2 g
80 g Brussel sprouts	0.135 g

BREAKFAST
AND BRUNCH

WHETHER YOU LIKE YOUR
BREAKFAST SWEET, SAVOURY,
SOLO, FOR TWO, ON-THE-GO
OR LATE 'N' LAZY, THERE'S A
FLAVOURSOME VEGETARIAN
OPTION FOR YOU.

Pea and mint omelette

This recipe is the perfect mix of fresh flavour and substance, plus you start the day with a nice hit of protein.

Serves 1

INGREDIENTS:

3 medium eggs

25 g peas

knob of butter or non-dairy substitute

3 mint leaves, torn

Whisk the eggs together until the yolk is fully combined with the white.

Boil water and pour over the peas so they partially cook (if peas are frozen, place in a pan and boil for 2 mins).

Melt knob of butter in a small frying pan and pour eggs in.

When the omelette is starting to set, scatter peas over and cook for a further 3 minutes.

Fold omelette over and scatter mint leaves on top to serve.

ANIMALS ARE MY FRIENDS... AND I DON'T EAT MY FRIENDS.

GEORGE BERNARD SHAW

All About Vegetarianism

The food consumed by the world's cattle is equal to the calorific needs of 8.7 billion people – over a billion more than the world's current human population.

The best breakfast in the world

This egg recipe is the perfect start to your day: a little bundle of protein, iron, vitamins and low-sugar carbs. Plus it's super tasty, so you know you're starting the day off on the right foot.

Serves 1

INGREDIENTS:

sourdough

1 egg

1 tbsp olive oil

50 g spinach

butter or non-dairy substitute

pepper to taste

Lightly grill or toast a slice of sourdough.

Meanwhile, bring a pan of water to simmer. Break your

egg into a cup or ramekin and, stirring the water, pour into the centre of the pan. This should help the white form around the yolk. Poach for 4 minutes.

Heat a tablespoon of olive oil in a small frying pan on a low heat and wilt the spinach. This shouldn't take long – just enough time for you to butter your toast.

Heap the spinach on your sourdough then top with poached egg.

Grind pepper to taste.

Breakfast burrito

When you gotta go, you gotta go, so if you've gotta get up and go in the morning grab this wrap and take it with you. You can adapt this recipe for other meals too – simply top a bowl of rice with the prepared black beans and you have a wonderful dinner. For best results, prepare the beans the evening before and reheat in the morning.

Serves 2

INGREDIENTS:

1 tbsp vegetable oil

1 onion, diced finely

5 cloves garlic, crushed then chopped

1 red bell pepper, sliced thinly

3 bay leaves

½ tsp salt

400 g tin black beans

1 tsp soy sauce

2 eggs

knob of butter or non-dairy alternative

2 flour tortillas

2 handfuls grated cheese

1 large avocado, sliced

Heat the oil and fry the onion and garlic in a medium-sized frying pan on a medium heat until the onion is translucent. Add the pepper and fry until softened.

Add the bay leaves, salt and black beans (including the liquid from the tin) and simmer for at least 45 minutes. If the black beans start to look dry add a splash of water but not so much they turn into a little stew. When done stir in the soy sauce. The longer you cook the beans the more flavoursome they will be.

Crack the eggs into a bowl and whisk until white and yolk are combined. Melt a knob of butter on a low heat in a small, separate frying pan and stir in the eggs. Leave for one minute so they start to cook and then stir as they firm then remove from heat.

Lay the tortillas flat and sprinkle a handful of cheese on each. Split the egg between the two and add several spoonfuls of beans (the wraps need to be full but able to close, so measure this by eye). Finally, layer sliced avocado in the middle.

Wrap the tortillas burrito-style to keep everything in and you're ready to go!

UNTIL HE EXTENDS HIS CIRCLE OF COMPASSION TO INCLUDE ALL LIVING THINGS, MAN WILL NOT HIMSELF FIND PEACE.

ALBERT SCHWEITZER

All About Vegetarianism

Famous vegetarians and vegans include Ellen DeGeneres, Paul McCartney, Ariana Grande, Jane Goodall and Natalie Portman.

Avocado and mango smash

Bring the tropics to your table with this bright slice of zingy fruity flavour. Sourdough or ciabatta are good options for this recipe as they are both strong, crusty breads that will be able to support the weight of the topping (you want a breakfast smash, not a breakfast splat).

Serves 1

INGREDIENTS:

1 ripe medium avocado

1 ripe mango, cut into chunks

½ lime

1 slice crusty bread

Scoop the avocado and mango into a bowl.

Squeeze the lime juice on top of the avocado and mango

and mix. Gently stir with a spoon for a chunky topping or combine using a fork for a creamy smash that's almost a mash.

Grill the bread on both sides until lightly toasted.

Top the warm bread with your avocado and mango mixture.

The-morning-after fry-up

Let's address those vegetarian fears head on: you don't have to give up fry ups just because you've said goodbye to meat. If anything, they've just got better! Veggie sausages are a healthier option than – and as tasty as – meat sausages, and halloumi replaces bacon as the salty element on the plate.

Serves 2

INGREDIENTS:

2 tbsp vegetable oil

1 large tomato, halved

150 g mushrooms, sliced

4 meat-free sausages

225 g pack halloumi, sliced thickly

2 eggs

200 g tin baked beans

2 slices of bread

butter or non-dairy alternative

Preheat the grill to a medium heat.

Heat 1 tbsp oil in a large frying pan and toss the tomato halves in it until fully coated. Let sit for ten minutes on a medium heat and add the mushrooms.

Cook mushrooms for around 10 minutes until reduced, then push to edge of the pan. Flip the tomatoes and add 1 tbsp oil and the sausages. Check the tomatoes and remove from heat, storing in foil, if they are ready. Fry sausages according to pack instructions, usually 10–12 minutes.

When you put the sausages on, layer a grill tray with the halloumi and grill on a medium heat. Turn sausages and halloumi after five minutes and add the eggs to the pan.

When you have two minutes left on the sausages and halloumi, heat the beans and pop the bread in the toaster.

Loading up your plate can take a bit of juggling. Start with the grilled items as they will retain their heat as you add your other bits to the plate. Pour the beans and add the toast last, spreading on a quick slick of butter.

I HAVE NO DOUBT THAT IT IS A PART OF THE DESTINY OF THE HUMAN RACE, IN ITS GRADUAL IMPROVEMENT, TO LEAVE OFF EATING ANIMALS.

HENRY DAVID THOREAU

Tropical breakfast smoothie bowl

Breakfast doesn't have to be complicated to be off the hook delicious! And you don't have to be a vegetarian to enjoy a smoothie bowl but while you're here, you might as well see everything that the beautiful world of fresh fruit has to offer.

Serves 1

INGREDIENTS:

½ banana

200 ml frozen mango and pineapple

150 ml coconut water

1 tbsp honey plus extra for drizzling

sunflower seeds

granola

1 nectarine, sliced

Blitz the banana, frozen fruit, coconut water and honey together in a blender until smooth. Check the consistency: if you would like it a little thicker, add the remaining banana.

Pour into a bowl and stripe with sunflower seeds, granola and sliced nectarine.

Drizzle a little honey over everything.

Hash-up

This recipe is perfect for hosting brunch. Take your pan of hash straight from the hob to the table and everyone can dig in – although it's all very pally until someone steals the bit you had your eye on!

Serves 2

INGREDIENTS:

500 g small potatoes, peeled and diced

enough vegetable oil to cover the base of a frying pan

1 red onion, diced

2 roasted red bell peppers, sliced thinly

100 g feta

2 eggs

pepper

parsley, chopped

Boil the potatoes for ten minutes, then drain and pat dry.

Heat the oil in a pan. Use one potato piece for testing: if it sizzles when you add it to the pan, the oil is ready.

Add the potatoes and fry for 15 minutes, tossing occasionally to ensure all sides are crispy.

Remove the potatoes and drain the oil. The base of the pan should still be coated with sufficient oil to cook the remaining ingredients.

Add the onion and cook on a low heat until soft. Return the potatoes to the pan and add the red pepper. Toss to combine.

Crumble the feta over the mixture and toss again. Make two small wells in the mixture and crack an egg in each well. Cover pan with a lid and leave until eggs have firmed up.

Season with pepper and parsley, then serve in the pan.

All About Vegetarianism

The first Vegetarian Society in the Western world was formed in England in 1847. At the time the members viewed vegetarianism as a form of temperance, omitting meat alongside alcohol (luckily, this is not a modern-day restriction).

LUNCH AND SNACK IDEAS

BREAK THE BOREDOM OF THE
DULL LUNCHTIME SANDWICH
AND EMBRACE YOUR VEGETARIAN
WILD SIDE. THESE EASY,
FILLING, EXCITING MEALS AND
PICKY BITS WILL ENLIVEN
ANY AFTERNOON'S MEAL.

Panzanella

This isn't your garden-variety garden salad; this is a big, indulgent, soaked, filling bowlful of herbs, veg and bread that proves that salad can be sexy. It works best with overripe tomatoes and day-old bread, so it's also perfect for using up food that's past its best.

Serves 4

INGREDIENTS:

6 medium tomatoes, halved

4 garlic cloves, sliced thickly

4 slices stale crusty bread

12 cm chunk cucumber, chopped

1 red onion, diced

1 tbsp flat leaf parsley, chopped

10 tbsp olive oil

2 tbsp white wine vinegar (cider vinegar and sherry vinegar can be used as substitutes)

small bunch basil, torn

4 tbsp capers, rinsed

Preheat the oven to 180°C. Pierce the tomatoes, slide the garlic chunks inside and roast for 1 hour, until slightly dried.

Meanwhile, heat grill or griddle pan and lightly toast the bread. A few char marks add to the taste and the look of the salad.

Tear bread into pieces in large bowl.

Add tomatoes, cucumber, onion and parsley. Drizzle with the oil and vinegar, and toss.

Leave to sit for 1 hour minimum. Add basil and capers before serving.

IF WE'RE DESTROYING OUR TREES
AND HURTING OUR ENVIRONMENT
AND HURTING ANIMALS AND
HURTING ONE ANOTHER AND ALL
THAT STUFF, THERE'S GOT TO BE
A VERY POWERFUL ENERGY TO
FIGHT THAT. I THINK WE NEED
MORE LOVE IN THE WORLD.

ELLEN DeGENERES

Simple batter

If you're not a health nut then a diet consisting of mainly vegetables might be a little galling. But even vegetables can be made indulgently delicious! This simple batter is easy to whip up and you can use it for all occasions, from tempura to tapas.

Serves 1

INGREDIENTS:

180 ml sparkling water, chilled

150 g self-raising flour

1 tsp paprika (optional)

1 tsp fine black pepper (optional)

vegetable oil, enough to submerge your
   battered vegetables in

chopped vegetables, see serving suggestions

Pour the water into the flour, paprika and pepper, whisking with a fork as you go.

The consistency should be light and runny but thick enough to cling to the vegetables – it's OK to have lumps.

Heat your oil on a high heat until simmering. (Never leave boiling oil unattended as it is a fire risk.)

Dip your veggies into the batter and fry for at least two minutes on each side. It's best to do this in batches so they cook evenly and you don't overcrowd the pan.

Thicker-cut veggies will need longer – fry one battered vegetable first as a test.

SERVING SUGGESTIONS:

Cut two aubergines into 5-mm thick rounds and serve drizzled in honey for a classic tapas plate. Add the paprika to this recipe.

Cut four stalks of asparagus into 2-cm sticks, and half a courgette into 5-mm thick rounds and serve with a zingy onion or tomato chutney. Add the pepper to this recipe.

Cut halloumi into thick strips and serve with chunky chips for a vegetarian's fish 'n' chips. Add the pepper to this recipe.

Cut a red bell pepper into 2-cm chunks and a head of broccoli into small florets to make tempura. Serve with a soy and spring onion dipping sauce.

Fresh quesadillas

This recipe is infinitely customizable and easily scaled down or up, depending on what you have in your cupboards and how many people you're feeding. As long as you have something spicy, something fresh, and something creamy you can put almost anything in your quesadilla and it will blow your socks off.

Serves 4

INGREDIENTS:

pack mock chicken chunks or strips
pack smoky BBQ fajita mix
½ red onion
1 tbsp vegetable oil
8 flour tortillas
2 tbsp chipotle paste
10 jarred jalapeños, chopped finely
small bunch coriander, chopped finely
2 handfuls grated cheese

Cook mock chicken according to instructions on the pack, usually around 12 minutes, adding fajita mix for the final two minutes. Put to one side.

Chop onion into half-moon slices.

Heat a large frying pan with a small amount of oil, spreading with a bit of paper towel to ensure pan is fully coated.

Meanwhile lay out a tortilla. Spread a knife tip's worth of chipotle over half of the tortilla. Add up to five bits of onion (raw onion can be quite powerful so this is to taste).

Scatter over a pinch of jalapeño chunks, handful of coriander and small handful of chicken substitute. Cover with grated cheese. The more filling you have the more cheese you will need as this is what melts and holds the quesadilla together.

Fold the clean half of the tortilla over the fillings and add to the pan. You should be able to cook two in one pan once you get the hang of it.

Fry until golden and crispy on one side, occasionally pressing down on top with a spatula to ensure the two sides stick together. Flip and repeat.

Repeat the filling and frying stages until all tortillas are cooked.

All About Vegetarianism

Historically vegetarianism has a link with utopias. One of the earliest feminist novels, *Herland* by Charlotte Perkins Gilman, imagines a utopia that includes vegetarianism.

Shakshuka

Serve this dish in the pan and use warm flatbread to scoop up all the deliciousness.

Serves 2

INGREDIENTS:

½ tsp cumin seeds

1 tbsp vegetable oil

2 red bell peppers, sliced into strips

2 green bell peppers, sliced into strips

½ tsp coriander

1 tsp cumin powder

½ tsp mild chilli powder

bunch coriander, stalks chopped finely and leaves chopped roughly

2 x 400 g can chopped tomatoes

2 tbsp tomato paste

100 g feta cheese

4 eggs

You will need a large frying pan with a lid or that can go under the grill for this recipe.

Fry the cumin seeds without oil for 1–2 minutes, until they start to pop and release their smell. Remove from the pan.

Heat 1 tbsp oil and fry the pepper for around 10 minutes, until soft and floppy. Stir in the coriander, cumin and chilli powder and fry for a further 3 minutes.

Stir in the coriander stalks, chopped tomatoes and tomato paste and simmer until thickened, at least 10 minutes.

Crumble the feta evenly over the mix and grill for 5 minutes.

Make four wells in the sauce and break an egg into each well. Depending on your pan, either place the lid on the pan or place the pan under the grill.

When the egg is cooked to your liking (usually 3 minutes for the albumen to turn white) take off the heat.

Top with coriander leaves and serve in the pan.

EATING FOR ME IS HOW
YOU PROCLAIM YOUR
BELIEFS THREE TIMES A
DAY... THREE TIMES A DAY,
I REMIND MYSELF THAT I
VALUE LIFE AND DO NOT
WANT TO CAUSE PAIN TO OR
KILL OTHER LIVING BEINGS.

NATALIE PORTMAN

Bruschetta

Serves 4

INGREDIENTS:

2 garlic cloves
150 g cherry tomatoes, quartered
handful basil leaves, torn
glug of olive oil
1 half baguette

Peel and mince one of the garlic cloves and mix with the tomatoes, basil and olive oil.

Cut the baguette into thin rounds and grill on both sides until lightly toasted.

Peel the second garlic clove and halve. Using a sharp knife, score lines onto one flat side of the baguette rounds. Rub with the garlic.

While bread is still warm, heap with the tomato and basil mix.

All About Vegetarianism

Lord Byron, Percy Bysshe Shelley, Voltaire and Leo Tolstoy were all notable early champions of vegetarianism.

Falafel wraps

Dry, crumbly, shop-bought falafel has besmirched falafel's good name for too long! Make your own at home and it will be fluffy, soft *and* cheap. If that's not enough, falafel is a great source of protein. You can make a batch at the weekend and use them for easy lunches during the week.

Serves 1

INGREDIENTS:

For the falafel

400 g can chickpeas, drained

2 cloves garlic

50 g fresh parsley, chopped finely

1 small red onion, chopped roughly

1 tsp powdered coriander

1 tsp powdered cumin

½ tsp chilli powder

squeeze lemon

2 tbsp vegetable oil (for frying)

To assemble

small tub hummus

pack of khubz flatbreads

2 large tomatoes, diced

2 roasted red bell peppers, sliced thinly

1–3 pepperoncini chillies, cut into rounds (optional)

bunch spring onions, stems and heads chopped

½ bunch coriander, including stalks, chopped finely

Mash the falafel ingredients (except oil) together until the mixture is combined and crumbly but still has lumps in.

Split the mixture into 8 portions and pat into balls.

Heat the oil in a frying pan and fry in batches, turning the falafel until crispy all over.

Spread a thin layer of hummus on a khubz

Chop a couple of falafels in half and lay them in a line on the left half of the khubz. Sprinkle over a handful of spring onions and coriander.

Spread several chunks of tomato, slices of pepper and chillies (if using) over the remaining khubz.

Starting from the left, roll up the khubz. The falafel should be in the centre of the wrap, surrounded by layers of flatbread and filling.

THE SOUL IS THE SAME IN ALL LIVING CREATURES, ALTHOUGH THE BODY OF EACH IS DIFFERENT.

HIPPOCRATES

Buddha bowl

Load these bowls up correctly and you'll get a serious hit of nutrition paired with a serious hit of deliciousness.

Serves 2

INGREDIENTS:

1 large sweet potato, peeled and chopped into cubes

1 can chickpeas, drained

1 tsp vegetable oil

½ tsp garlic powder

1 tsp mild curry powder

½ tsp turmeric

salt and pepper to taste

140 g quinoa, cooked

several leaves purple cabbage, shredded

several handfuls of spring greens, shredded

1 lemon, zested and juiced

2 tsp olive oil

100 g hummus

Preheat the oven to 190°C.

Toss the sweet potato and chickpeas in 1 tsp oil, with garlic powder, curry powder, turmeric, salt and pepper to taste.

Roast for 30 minutes, tossing the ingredients halfway through the time.

Portion the quinoa and shredded cabbage into two bowls.

Meanwhile boil the spring greens for 5 minutes and drain. Mix zest and juice of 1 lemon with olive oil and toss greens in the mix. Add greens to bowls.

Quarter the remaining lemon and add to bowls with large dollop of hummus.

Remove sweet potato and chickpeas from oven, add to the bowls and serve.

WHAT'S FOR DINNER?

HERE IS A MIX OF EASY-TO-MAKE
WEEKDAY MEALS AND FANCY
DISHES THAT ARE GREAT FOR
WEEKENDS AND HOSTING GUESTS.

WE CANNOT HAVE
PEACE AMONG MEN
WHOSE HEARTS FIND
DELIGHT IN KILLING ANY
LIVING CREATURE.

RACHEL CARSON

Mushroom puff tart

This is a great dish to serve at a party because it's quick to make and looks fantastic! Of course, it tastes great too; the soft, creamy mushroom and spinach filling contrasting nicely with the crisp pastry shell and the freshness of the rocket.

Serves 4

INGREDIENTS:

50 g butter

2 packs puff pastry sheets

6 large portobello mushrooms, sliced

3 cloves garlic, finely diced

½ tbsp thyme leaves

150 g baby spinach

pinch of nutmeg, freshly grated

250 g blue cheese, roughly crumbled

100 g rocket

handful pine nuts

Preheat oven to 180°C, grease and line baking tray with baking paper. Melt half the butter over a gentle heat.

Take pastry sheets and cut in half. Create the sides of the pastry case by cutting 1 cm diagonals into the corners. Fold the edges over and press down lightly.

Brush border you have created with melted butter. Take the top left and bottom right corners, and pull them over the sheet to meet their opposite corners. This should create a 'pie case' effect. Brush border again with melted butter and bake for 15 minutes until golden brown.

Meanwhile, melt remaining butter. Sauté the mushrooms with garlic then stir in thyme leaves. Wilt spinach leaves over mixture. Grate pinch of nutmeg over spinach as it wilts. Stir in cheese and cook for 2 minutes until slightly melted.

Spoon into cases and bake for 5 minutes. Top with rocket and pine nuts, and serve.

Lemony kedgeree

Kedgeree is traditionally made with smoked fish and this vegetarian version includes smoked paprika to recreate the smoky flavour. The lemon wedges are a must – their sharpness combines with the fresh ginger and cuts through the sweetness of the cardamom and the spice of the turmeric and curry. Between the eggs, spinach and kale you're getting nearly half of your daily calcium, iron, protein and zinc.

Serves 2

INGREDIENTS:

1 tbsp vegetable oil

small bunch spring onions

2 garlic cloves, minced

4 cardamom pods, crushed

1 thumb-sized piece of
    ginger, grated

1 tsp mild curry powder

pinch chilli flakes

¼ tsp smoked paprika

½ tsp turmeric

200 g long grain or
    basmati rice

800 ml veg stock

4 eggs

200 g kale, chopped

200g spinach, tough
   stalks removed

1 tsp vegetable oil

lemon quarters, to serve

Heat 1 tbsp oil in a pan and add onions, frying gently for 2 minutes.

Add garlic, cardamom, ginger, curry powder, chilli flakes, paprika and turmeric. Fry for 1 minute and then stir in rice and fry for further 2 minutes.

Add the stock and bring to the boil, then simmer until the rice is cooked, around 20 minutes.

Meanwhile boil eggs for 8 minutes, drain and place in a bowl of cold water.

Add kale to the rice pan and cook for 2 minutes. Add the spinach and cook for a further 3 minutes.

Peel eggs and quarter them. Serve the kedgeree topped with egg and lemon quarters.

Lentil stew

This is cheap and easy comfort food at its finest. It's hard to believe that a dish this easy to prepare can be as tasty as it is – and contain as much essential protein, fibre and iron – but try it and find out!

Serves 2

INGREDIENTS:

1 tbsp vegetable oil

1 onion, chopped finely

2 cloves garlic, minced

400 g tin green lentils

400 g tin chopped tomatoes

2 tbsp sundried tomato puree

2 tbsp Italian mixed herbs (optional)

4 veggie sausages

Heat the oil in a large, heavy-bottomed pan and cook the onion on a low-to-medium heat until softened and translucent.

Add the garlic and fry for a further two minutes, then pour in the lentils and tomatoes.

Stir to combine. Add the tomato puree (and if the puree does not contain additional herbs, add the herbs) and simmer.

Meanwhile fry the veggie sausages for 10 minutes then chop into chunks and add to the lentil stew.

Simmer until sauce is thickened, stirring occasionally.

All About Vegetarianism

Stricter variations of veganism include fruitarianism and raw veganism, which is a vegan diet with all food eaten in its raw state. A fruitarian diet is made up of at least 75 per cent fruit, the other 25 per cent made up of seeds and nuts. It can be hard to maintain the right nutritional balance on a fruitarian diet so it is not suitable for children, pregnant women and teens.

Orange tofu

For an extra-fresh flavour, squeeze the orange juice yourself from fresh oranges. It's a little bit of extra work but a lot-tle extra zest in your mouth. This recipe has the indulgence of a take-away dish with very nearly as little effort.

Serves 2

INGREDIENTS:

1 pack firm tofu

1 ½ tbsp cornflour plus more to coat

200 ml orange juice

75 g brown sugar

1 tbsp soy sauce

thumb-sized piece of fresh ginger, grated

2 garlic cloves minced

1 tsp orange zest

1 or 2 tbsps vegetable oil (for frying)

2 spring onions, chopped

pinch sesame seeds

Drain the liquid from the tofu and press it for at least 20 minutes.

Meanwhile, combine 1 ½ tbsp cornflour in 2 tbsp of the orange juice. Set aside.

Add the remaining orange juice, the brown sugar, soy sauce, ginger, garlic and orange zest to a small saucepan. Stir to combine. Bring the mixture to boil on a high heat and then reduce to a medium heat and let simmer for 15 minutes.

Add the cornflour mixture and stir until completely blended. Set aside.

Chop the tofu into 2-cm cubes and toss gently in remaining cornflour to coat.

Heat the vegetable oil (the oil should coat the base of a large frying pan). Add the tofu and fry for 2 minutes on each side until they are golden and crispy all over, with a soft inside.

Add the sauce and toss to coat.

Serve topped with spring onions and sesame seeds.

I FEEL SO MUCH HAPPIER NOT BEING A PART OF THE BLOOD CHAIN.

JOANNA LUMLEY

Mexican halloumi skewers

Serves 4

INGREDIENTS:

2 tbsp sunflower oil

good grind of pepper

1 lime, juiced

1 tbsp honey

2 tbsp chipotle fajita mix

handful coriander, chopped finely

500 g halloumi, chopped into chunks

3 mixed bell peppers, chopped into chunks

2 large red onions, chopped into chunks

1 lime, quartered

Blitz the oil, pepper, lime juice, honey, fajita mix and coriander together until combined.

Pour into a bowl and toss the halloumi, pepper and onion

in it until coated, then leave to marinate in the fridge for at least 30 mins.

Pre-heat the grill.

Alternating halloumi, pepper and onion, load your skewers with at least two of each ingredient.

Grill on a medium heat for 5 mins each side, until the veggies are charred.

Load up the skewers onto a plate and pour any remaining marinade over them.

Serve with wedges of lime and a rice dish for a full meal.

Aloo tikki with two dipping sauces

Aloo tikki are spiced potato patties usually served as part of an appetizer plate but serve well as a light bite for dinner if you're not too hungry. They're great for chipping away at that pack of peas that seems to linger in the freezer for all eternity.

Serves 4 (small plates)

INGREDIENTS:

<u>For the aloo tikki:</u>

4 large potatoes, peeled and chopped

200 g peas

8 tbsp breadcrumbs

1 tbsp cornflour

1 thumb-sized piece of ginger, grated

handful of coriander leaves and stems, chopped finely

2 green chillies, chopped finely

1 tsp garam masala powder

1 tsp chilli powder

1 tsp lemon juice

1 tbsp vegetable oil

For the white dipping sauce:

100 ml natural yoghurt

1 thumb-sized piece of ginger, grated

4 spring onions, chopped

1 tbsp lemon juice

For the green dipping sauce:

bunch coriander, leaves and stems roughly chopped

3 green chillies, chopped roughly

1 tbsp lemon juice

1 tsp sugar

1 tsp salt

1 tbsp olive oil

1 thumb-sized piece of ginger, peeled and roughly chopped

Boil the potatoes until soft and then mash them until smooth. Mix in the peas, 4 tbsp of the breadcrumbs and the remaining ingredients (aside from the oil) until combined.

Divide the mixture into around 10–14 equal parts and roll into golf-ball-sized balls. Flatten to make 1 cm-thick patties.

Pour the remaining breadcrumbs onto a plate. Coat the patties by pressing them to the plate, first one side then the other.

Heat 1 tbsp oil in a pan and add 4 patties. Fry one side and then the other until golden brown. Remove from the pan and keep under tinfoil to keep warm and repeat with other patties.

Meanwhile make the dipping sauces. For the white dipping sauce: mix the yoghurt, ginger, white bits of the spring onion and lemon juice. Top with the green bits of the spring onion.

For the green sauce: blitz together all the ingredients. The result should be smooth and liquid; if it is dry add a little more oil or lemon juice (lemon juice will increase the acidity so only do this if you like tangy flavours).

When all patties are ready, serve with the sauces.

All About Vegetarianism

Religions that adhere to a vegetarian diet include Hinduism, Mahayana Buddhism and Seventh-day Adventist Christianity.

Thai green curry

If you make a big batch of the paste then you can keep any leftovers in the freezer and give yourself a head start on a delicious dinner.

Serves 4

INGREDIENTS:

<u>For the paste:</u>

1 stalk lemongrass, minced

1–3 Thai green chillies, sliced

1 shallot, sliced

4–5 cloves garlic

1 thumb-size piece of ginger, sliced thinly

150 g coriander, chopped

150 g fresh basil

½ tsp ground cumin

½ tsp ground white pepper

½ tsp ground coriander

1 tbsp soy sauce

1 tsp salt

2 tbsp lime juice

1 tsp brown sugar

3–4 tbsp coconut milk (enough to blend ingredients together)

For the curry:

800 g mixed veg, sliced; could include mushroom, courgette, aubergine, carrot, onion, pepper, green beans.

400 ml tin coconut milk

2 tbsp vegetable oil

Whizz together the ingredients in a blender for the paste.

Heat 2 tbsp oil and fry the veg (apart from any fast-cooking veg such as green beans) for 5 minutes.

Add the paste and fry for a further 2 minutes.

Stir in the coconut milk and bring to the boil, add any fast-cooking veg such as green beans, then simmer for 10 minutes.

Serve with rice.

Crispy chilli veggie beef

Serves 4

INGREDIENTS:

1 pack veggie mince

3 tbsp cornflour

2 tsp Chinese five spice

100 ml vegetable oil, plus 50 ml spare

1 red bell pepper, sliced thinly

1 red chilli, halved, deseeded and sliced thinly

small bunch spring onions, chopped

3 garlic cloves, diced finely

1 thumb-sized piece of ginger, cut into matchsticks

4 tbsp rice wine vinegar

1 tbsp soy sauce

2 tbsp sweet chilli sauce

2 tbsp tomato ketchup

3 dried noodle nests

Toss the mince in the cornflour and five spice until coated.

Heat the oil and add the mince. Toss briefly and then leave for 5 minutes so the mince starts to crisp up. Flip and fry on the other side until the mince is covered in crispy bits. Veggie mince is very absorbent, so you may need to add more oil to prevent the pan from getting too dry and burning.

Remove mince from the pan and pat dry.

If the pan is dry, heat 1 tbsp oil. Stir fry the pepper, half the chilli, white spring onion, garlic and ginger for 3 mins on a high heat.

Meanwhile boil noodles and drain when done.

Combine the vinegar, soy sauce, sweet chilli sauce and ketchup and pour into the frying pan. Allow to start to boil, then add the mince back to the pan. Toss to combine ingredients and coat mince.

Top noodles with mince and scatter green spring onion ends and remaining chilli to serve.

WE ALL LOVE ANIMALS. WHY DO WE CALL SOME 'PETS' AND OTHERS 'DINNER'?

K. D. LANG

Veggie chilli

Serves 4

INGREDIENTS:

2 tbsp vegetable oil

2 red onions, diced

3 garlic cloves, crushed

2 chillies, chopped finely

bunch coriander, stalks and leaves
   separated and chopped finely

400 ml passata

1 tbsp chipotle paste

240 g tin kidney beans

350 g packet veggie mince

1 tsp mild chilli powder

1 tsp smoked paprika

small tub sour cream

small sourdough loaf, optional

Heat 1 tbsp oil in a pan and fry onions, garlic, chillies and coriander stems for 3 minutes.

Stir in passata, chipotle paste and kidney beans and simmer on a medium heat.

Meanwhile, in a separate pan, heat 1 tbsp oil and fry the vegetarian mince for 10 minutes. Add chilli powder and paprika and fry for a further 2 minutes.

Stir mince into the sauce and simmer until the sauce is thickened. Just before serving stir in ¾ of the coriander leaves.

If you're feeling fancy, hollow out the sourdough loaf and serve chilli in that, with the removed bread on the side for dipping. Otherwise serve alone or with rice and a good dollop of sour cream. Sprinkle the remaining coriander on top to garnish.

All About Vegetarianism

In India, vegetarians and vegans make up around 40 per cent of the population.

HINTS
AND TIPS

Now that you've learned about the basics of vegetarianism, here are a few hints and tips to help you make the most of a vegetarian lifestyle. Learn about the common food and household items that contain 'hidden' animal products and discover even more information about how to eat well as a vegetarian.

ALTERNATIVE MEATS

Alternative meats are having a bit of a gala moment. Vegetarians are no longer limited to tofu and a bean burger from a speciality shop, but can find a wide variety of meat replacements in most supermarkets. Most veggie meat is modelled after an animal meat product, using flavour and texture to imitate the eating experience. The most common products include chicken pieces, chicken cutlets, sausages, burgers and 'beef mince', but you can also easily find chorizo, pepperoni, steak cutlets, steak strips, duck, pulled pork, ham slices, turkey slices, fish, battered prawns, chicken nuggets, bacon and more. One of the easiest ways to transition to a vegetarian diet is to make some of your favourite dishes but replace the meat with veggie meat. You'll need to check the recommended cooking time on the veggie meat packet as it's often quicker than meat, but otherwise you'll barely notice a difference (apart from bacon. We're still struggling a bit with bacon).

There isn't a standard ingredient to veggie meat; each company develops their own recipe for as nutritious and 'real feeling' a result as possible. A lot of products use soybean as a key ingredient as it's a great source of protein. Soy beans are a type of legume commonly used in Asian cooking; fermented soy beans are used to make soy sauce and tofu. One popular veggie meat company uses soil mould as a main ingredient, although you couldn't tell by looking at their products! Always check the packaging for nutritional information but you'll find that most veggie meats are a good source of protein, ably replacing the protein you would usually receive from animal meat.

DON'T BE JELLY OF MY JELLY

Gelatine is briefly touched upon on p.14 but here is a bit more information to help you make informed decisions about your gelatine intake. Be wary of any bouncy or wobbly food, as this is likely to contain gelatine. Most marshmallows and gummy sweets do – you're most likely to find vegetarian versions in specialist shops or online – although some sweets such as laces are more commonly gelatine-free. Set desserts such as jelly, panna cotta and some glazed, fruity cheesecakes often contain gelatine. If you're worried about missing out, don't be! Veggie alternatives to gelatine (usually pectin which is derived from fruit) are available in the baking aisle of most good supermarkets and although the method of preparation is different, the results are just as good.

SHELL, YEAH!

You may assume that shellac, if you've heard of it at all, is a type of long-lasting nail varnish. In fact, the varnish takes its name from its key ingredient; a resin secreted from the female lac insect. The process for collecting the resin scoops up most of the bugs as well so if you're using shellac you're using the bugs. Shellac is not only used in the production of nail varnish, but also in handlebar tape for bicycles, as a wood floor finish, as ink binder, as felt hat finisher, as a component of the fabric gossamer, in medication capsules and even as a coating on most supermarket citrus fruit.

If you're worried about shellac finding its way into your food and medication, keep an eye out for E904 on the packaging, which is the name of the additive. For loose citrus fruit that might be coated in it, contact the supermarket – they should have the information in their records. Other non-consumable products may not be as clear on whether they contain shellac as shellac nail varnish is so do check the packaging for details, or look online. There are a lot of vegan and vegetarian sites that highlight unexpected animal product use and suggest animal-free alternatives. PETA has an animal ingredients list on their website and Vegan Food & Living have a guide to spot hidden animal products on labels and packaging. If you're still unclear, contact the manufacturers, who should be able to tell you more.

LEATHER HEAD

Leather replacements are already in popular circulation; materials such as pleather are well known and often used on low-cost shoes and accessories. Check the label of the item you are buying for information on the material; the information is usually readily available. However, many leather replacements are not environmentally-friendly, often containing plastic and using heaps of petroleum in the process. If that's a concern for you, several companies are creating eco-conscious leathers using cork, slate, paper or plant materials such as bark or bush.

VEGETARIAN MEDICINES

Medicine is an area that can trip up even experienced vegetarians and vegans. Lots of medicines involve some sort of animal product. This book recommends that you always prioritise your personal well-being and only make health decisions with the aid of your doctor. However, educating yourself on the animal products contained in medicines can help you have that discussion with your health practitioner.

Capsule tablets often contain either gelatine or shellac in their casing, so vegetarians and vegans may choose to opt for solid pills where they can, particularly in easily-available over-the-counter medications such as pain relief. Be aware that some solid pills still use gelatine to bind the pill together, so check your packaging.

Hormonal tablets, such as birth control pills, menopause treatments or insulin, contain lactose, which is a carrier for the active medicine. Lactose is derived from milk and sometimes calf rennet; technically the former is acceptable for vegetarians but the latter (rennet is fat) is certainly not.

Magnesium stearate is a product that is sometimes derived from animal fats (and sometimes from plants) and is used to bind tablets together.

Finally, it must be said that no medicines are truly animal-cruelty-free. In almost all countries world-wide a pharmaceutical medicine must have been tested on an animal before being tested on humans, ahead of being approved for use.

IF NOT MEAT THEN WHAT?

Vegetarian cooking can take a little getting used to as most people usually structure their meals around the meat. If you're still adapting and you need something to swap the meat out for, try 'chunky' veg such as thick slices of aubergine, courgette, squash, portobello mushroom or cauliflower. See the next tip for advice on how to prepare these ingredients. Switching to all-in-one dishes such as risottos, curries and noodles can also help ease the transition while you get used to subbing in non-meat meat. There is also, of course, mock meat (p.108–9) if you still want the impression of eating meat. Ease yourself in with mock meats such as breaded chicken bits, sausages and burgers as these often run the closest in taste and texture to their animal-product counterparts.

DON'T JUST BOIL 'EM, MASH 'EM, STICK 'EM IN A STEW

The fact of the matter is, now that meat is no longer the star of the show it's time for vegetables to shine. I don't want to make assumptions about your pre-vegetarian life but a lot of omnivore cooking focuses on prepping the meat, plopping a few boiled vegetables or a green salad on the plate as an accompaniment. I just want to say, *it gets better*.

Firstly, roasted vegetables are not just for Sunday dinner. There are precious few vegetables that aren't delicious after a good roasting – some crisp round the edges, some soft and slightly charred, others caramelised. Even something as simple as swapping your saucepan for a roasting tin can improve your vegetable experience.

If you don't have time to roast, how about chargrilling the veg? You'll still get the smoky, slightly charred flavour, but more quickly.

Consider how you've dressed your vegetables. As someone wise probably once said, every time you close a flavour door, you open a flavour window. A few spices and fresh herbs can revolutionise any dish, and a squeeze of lemon or lime can be applied to most dishes to lift the flavour. As an experiment, serve all your dishes topped with coriander, basil, parsley or chopped spring onion for a week (search online to see what herb pairs with which flavour) and see the improvement.

I CAN'T THINK OF ANYTHING BETTER IN THE WORLD TO BE BUT A VEGAN.

ALICIA SILVERSTONE

A vegetarian lifestyle goes a long way in preventing animal cruelty and helping the environment, but if you'd like to completely eliminate animal products from your life and do the best you can for the environment, a vegan lifestyle might be the best option for you. Here are a few answers to any vegan questions you might have, and a few tips to point you in the right direction if you want to transition from vegetarian to vegan.

WHY NOT MILK?

Many people say that they can understand the choice to be vegetarian, but that they don't see the problem with milk.

While it is true that milk does not directly kill the animal it is taken from, the dairy industry is, unfortunately, cruel. Cows are kept in confined conditions, even on organic farms, and repeatedly artificially inseminated to keep them producing milk. Their calves are taken from them seconds after birth – females to have the same fate as their mothers, and males usually to become veal.

Aside from the issue of cruelty, milk simply isn't designed for the human body. Cows' milk is intended to make a calf grow large quickly, not to add to the health of a human being. Approximately 75 per cent of the world's population is intolerant to lactose, and the calcium contained in milk can be hard for the human body to access because of the acidifying nature of milk. In short, milk is not a necessary addition to a balanced diet.

SHOULD I MAKE AN EGGCEPTION?

In many cultures, it is not considered vegetarian to eat eggs. The egg industry is cruel. Even 'free range' eggs generally come from hens who hardly see the light of day, live in cramped conditions, and have been bred to produce eggs at far beyond their natural rate, meaning their bodies wear out quickly, giving them short, unhappy lives. Male chicks fare worse; a worker 'sexes' them on hatching and if they are male and unable to lay eggs, they are killed.

Eggs are not a necessary food, and are not even needed for baking. It is simple to replace eggs in a cake and still have a moist and delicious treat. One answer is fruit. Don't worry, I'm not talking about having an apple when you're peckish. Mashed banana, for example, is a wonderful – and healthy – egg replacement, as is apple sauce. Juicy veg such as courgette or beetroot can also be whizzed up to make moist and spongy cakes. Flaxseed can be used as a binder too, and adds extra protein. Or, for a truly easy – if not as healthy – option, swap the eggs for oil.

OH HONEY

Honey is a subject of much debate, with some people who call themselves vegan still consuming it, along with other bee products such as honeycomb or bee pollen.

The reason honey is not considered vegan is primarily that it is an animal by-product, and that bees are exploited and often damaged by its production. Even small-sized producers and hobbyists often subject their bees to cruelty, such as cutting off the queen's wings so that she can't swarm.

If you want a sweet alternative to drizzle on your soya yoghurt, or to add to tea, try agave nectar, which comes from a cactus. Date syrup or rice syrup are also good alternatives.

SWEET TREATS

A big worry for people contemplating a vegan lifestyle is whether they will ever be able to enjoy sweet treats again. It's understandable; who doesn't love a sugary snack? If this taps into your darkest fears, don't worry; there is more out there than you might think.

If you're looking for pre-prepared sweets, scrutinise the wares on your supermarket shelves. There are lots of baked goods that swap butter for oil in order to cut costs and are therefore vegan-friendly. Frozen strudels and ready-made pastry are often vegan, as are some fruit pies. Many biscuits are 'accidentally' vegan, such as bourbon biscuits, hobnobs, party rings, some own-brand digestives and lotus biscuits. Some chocolate bars pass the test, too – Bournville, Fry's, and many minty dark-chocolate snacks just happen to be vegan.

If that still isn't enough, most shops sell specialist dairy-free chocolate for a reasonable price.

Conclusion

Perhaps you're now ready to take the plunge and become vegetarian; perhaps you've picked up a few good tips for your #meatfreeMondays. Whatever you choose, I hope that you walk away from this book feeling confident that vegetarianism is an easy-to-achieve lifestyle full of options, whether it's what food to eat or which shoes to buy. Congratulations on making the kinder choice for the environment, for our fellow animals and for yourself. Good luck on your vegetarian journey.

THE LITTLE BOOK
OF VEGANISM

Elanor Clarke

£5.99

Paperback

ISBN: 978-1-84953-759-9

There are plenty of reasons to embrace veganism – for environmental, ethical or health reasons, and many more! This easy-to-digest guide, packed with practical tips on vegan living, from food and drink to clothes and shopping, will inspire you to enjoy all that's best about an ethical animal-free lifestyle.

IMAGE CREDITS

If you're interested in finding out more about our books, find us on Facebook at **SUMMERSDALE PUBLISHERS** and follow us on Twitter at **@SUMMERSDALE**.

WWW.SUMMERSDALE.COM